People Poems
&
Other Poetry

George L. T. Wilks

BALBOA.PRESS
A DIVISION OF HAY HOUSE

Balboa Press books may be ordered through booksellers or by contacting:

Balboa Press
A Division of Hay House
1663 Liberty Drive
Bloomington, IN 47403
www.balboapress.com
844-682-1282

Because of the dynamic nature of the Internet, any web addresses or links contained in this book may have changed since publication and may no longer be valid. The views expressed in this work are solely those of the author and do not necessarily reflect the views of the publisher, and the publisher hereby disclaims any responsibility for them.

The author of this book does not dispense medical advice or prescribe the use of any technique as a form of treatment for physical, emotional, or medical problems without the advice of a physician, either directly or indirectly. The intent of the author is only to offer information of a general nature to help you in your quest for emotional and spiritual well-being. In the event you use any of the information in this book for yourself, which is your constitutional right, the author and the publisher assume no responsibility for your actions.

Any people depicted in stock imagery provided by Getty Images are models, and such images are being used for illustrative purposes only. Certain stock imagery © Getty Images.

Print information available on the last page.

ISBN: 978-1-9822-5774-3 (sc)
ISBN: 978-1-9822-5775-0 (e)

Balboa Press rev. date: 01/13/2021

Table of Contents

Daddy's Good-Bye 1

I'm Glad Your Mother's Genes Had Their Dominant Way 3

This Guy Named Lee Is A Hard Working Man.. 6

My Motherly Shining Star 8

Mom Is Always Ready, Mom Is Very Steady 9

Chim, Chim 11

Grandparent's Love 13

My Child 15

Dear Grace, My Love 16

The Story of the Unknown Plants 17

Eventually 18

Let Me 21

Talking About My Lady 22

My Love For You 23

Constantly Standing 24

Back In Those Days 26

You Are My Sun, I am The Rain 31

Shelly Became Ron's Ribbon In The Sky 32

My Only Lady, My Lovely Bride 36

What Can I say About Jesse & Pam? 38

To My Wife From Earl 40

Inner Beauty & Inner Qualities 41

A Wedding Anniversary Poetry Gift For Simon & Kattie Priester 42

Sovereign of the Seas Cruise Vacation 44

First One, Then the Other... 46

Coronavirus Known as Covid-19 48

Appreciating the "Elderly Ones" 50

A Living Trophy I will be.. 52

Pouring Rains of Blessings.. 53

The Holder of Our Existence Deed 54

My Eyes 55

Summer Breeze 56

Feverish Free Flight 57

Rushing Waves 58

Clouds... 59

This book of poetry is dedicated to my loving wife,
and my three beautiful daughters

My wife, Grace and me

My Daughters: in their teenage years
SHERYL, TAMIKA & CLAUDETTE

Preface

I AM A WRITER OF NON FICTIONAL NARRATIVE POETRY

I TELL STORIES ABOUT INDIVIDUALS

MY FAMILY,

CLOSE FRIENDS,

LIFE EXPERIENCES,

ASPIRATIONS,

AND OF A SPIRITUAL NATURE

THE INFATUATION THAT IS
BORN WITHIN ME
IS TO EXPRESS MYSELF
USING THE MEDIUM OF POETRY
TO STIR YOUR HEART AND MIND
WITH A GRACEFUL SOUND
NOT RELATING A SENSE
OF BEING VERY PROFOUND
RATHER, TO CONVEY A MESSAGE
WITH MEANING, RHYTHM AND RHYME
WRITING ABOUT LIFE'S EXPERIENCES
THAT INVOLVES PEOPLE OF DIFFERENT KINDS

Poems About People That Are
Part Of My Family Tree

This poem was written for my 2nd oldest daughter, Sheryl, in December of 1988. Shortly after graduating from high school she decided to move to California from our home in Cranford, NJ.

From our many vacation travels to the Los Angeles area over the past years while she was still in high school, she grew to love the area and told us that she would "one day move to L.A." She kept her goal.

Daddy's Good-Bye

It's almost time to part
and to say our good-byes

Knowing that you are leaving
May even bring tears to our eyes

But, please don't you fret
or feel sad or blue

Because we all support you
in moving, your desire to do

Although you'll be very far away
right here in my heart, close! You will always stay

Long since not an immature child
all grown up, with a personality and spirit
that's very quiet and mild

Especially knowing that you have the "Truth"
evident by your lifestyle, you have given me the proof

That no wrong temptation will ever sway
I'm confident you'll continue to walk in the true Christian way

Never forget your mother's unique touch
she too, dearly loves you so very much

She'll be constantly calling, asking you about that and this
remembering how you always washed the dishes
your helping hands in the kitchen she will surely miss

No brothers you have, but sisters numbering two
Claudette and Tamika, no more fussing with you

Relatives galore, little cousins and newphews all round
asking, where's Sherry going? She is California bound

And keep your east coast friends in mind
call or write them from time to time

However, **"Daddy's Good-Bye"** is not forever
It's just a figure of speech

For as long as we both are living
you are just an airplane's ride, five hours to reach

This poem was written for my youngest daughter, Tamika, in August of 1997. She was getting married during that month. And I wanted to express my inner most feelings for her on her very special wedding day.

I'm Glad Your Mother's Genes Had Their Dominant Way

Twenty six years ago was the start of something brand new
my wife and I thought long and hard! Is this something that we
really wanted to do?

We had our daughters that already numbered two
what if we took a third try, would a darling baby boy come through?

It seems as though my wife's genes were the stronger
but, I sincerely hoped that wasn't the case any much longer

On her side of the family, all girls her parent's did breed
inside my family clan the siblings boys took the lead
This time we thought that the male side would certainly win
and hoped I wouldn't experience anymore chagrin

As a firm decision was solemnly made
we trusted that all of the sperm would be a dominant male parade

As the nine months slowly passed away, it was my wholehearted plea
"dear God, bless me with a baby boy", I meant those words
so emphatically

But, on that 17th day of September, I was nervous, with much fright
as I got the news and I said to myself, "this just ain't right"
because my wife delivered another baby girl that fateful frantic night

But, as soon as that little female wonder came unto my unworthy sight, I forgot about what I really wanted, rather a great deal of joy and overwhelming delight

I, being the father, think God felt a little sympathy, because to my immense surprise this baby girl's face looked just like me!

To our lovely daughter & bride, Tamika. Regarding your birth on that notable day, **"I'm glad your mother's genes had their dominant way"**

However, in some ways my wish for a boy did, in fact, come true because as an infant you were doings things that little girls just shouldn't do

You were very daring, not quiet or even discreet. Always getting into something, you were an inquisitive terror on your little feet

Early on it seemed that you were for women's lib cause you made great escapes from your bedroom jailhouse crib

You were busy as a bumble bee or more like a little mole, whether night or in the day we found you gleefully playing in the household toilet bowl

As you grew older, your favorite things weren't dolls or toys you were more attuned to enjoying backyard games and playing with the boys

But as you aged and became physically older, your female hormones took control and your Tomboy days grew colder & colder. Yes, they were finally over!

Twenty six years have come and pass, gradually you became a mature women and now you are sealing your relationship with your man at last

So, stay by your commitment, your choice has been made
work together in faith, trust, and love
and your marriage and happiness will never, never fade

So, I'm very proud & happy on this, yours and Gary's wedding day,
"I'm glad your mother's genes had their dominant way"

This poem was written in March 1996 about my stepfather, Lee Merricks. He was an integral part of my life for many years. I wanted to honor him at his retirement party after working very hard for 44 years. Sadly, he passed away in 2007.

This Guy Named Lee Is A Hard Working Man

He migrated from the state of Florida, this guy named Lee
he came to reside in Rahway, a small town located in New Jersey

A good husband to Dolores, a devoted mother and wife, who brought
much renewed happiness and joy into his once dissatisfied life

Receiving her children along with his even before their marriage
began, it may have seemed more than he could handle, Rather than
stay, other men would have probably ran

He accepted this challenge with much love & his dedicated wedding
hand and won over big! Because **"this guy named Lee is a hard
working man"**

Employed as a warehouseman at a company called Cardinal China
no man was better for that job, no one will ever be finer

For over 44 years getting up early was his daily tradition
always fine tuned like a dependable subcompact car
to complete his assigned work mission

Well liked by all of his co-workers and overseers, cause he work hard
and proved himself during those early Cardinal China years

A truck trailer pulls up, a driver named Pat is bringing a shipment in
a humongous load for storage in the company's old brick building
within

This guy named Lee was lickety split. A rapid human sorter. Taking the elevator here and there, storing all those boxes of goods in some kind of logical numerical order

He picked & packed collector's doll items and a many Knick-knacks sending out the mail orders, right on time, like a finger pop snap!

All of the owners such as Sid, Charlie, & Sam, even the secretary, Sophie, all of them agree that **"this guy named Lee is a hard working man"**

Hey! Leroy! His company peers chose that name, he really didn't mind it, just so as long as they increased his wages, they didn't remain the same

And there was Allen & Gary, offspring of the senior's clan, as well as the money manager, Mike, I'm sure they all said it, **"this guy named Lee is a hard working man"**

Hoping that he would stay on forever and not take flight, cause those younger guys can't compare with his determined work ethic and unequaled physical might

Of course all of us know that a man can't work forever, the body is calling it restful due. So, that is why Lee decided to retire at the ripe age of sixty two

He well deserves it, so in our memories let it always stand!
"this guy named Lee is a hard working man"

This Poem is dedicated to my mother, Dolores Merricks

My Motherly Shining Star

These are the names of my nine siblings
Dennis, Frederick, Robert, Walter, Yvonne & Sharon

Then came along my stepbrothers; Wayne, Byron & Charlie
could it be, my mother felt sorry for all those women that were barren?

They all were brought into this world by Dolores, who is our mother
a total of ten children, equaling two sisters and eight brothers

Childbirth and rearing children are certainly hard things to do,
I really must say!
It is a full time job, worth more than any amount of monetary pay

My mother's longevity, into 2020, living now for 89 years
she is still going strong despite some physical ailments
without any hard pressed fears

I being the second oldest, know that it wasn't always easy for her
dealing with stress, strains, & early years living in poverty,
hard times did occur!

Despite that, she held true to her motherly instincts and obligations
as she built dedicated strong parenting foundations

I honor her for all that she did for us through all those financial hard times
never thinking about herself, leaving all of her untold inner desires behind

I truly thank her for the caring mother that she was and still are
In my heart and mind, she will always be my motherly shining star

Much Love,
George

This poem was written in November 1989 for my mother in law, Grace Barksdale. She was known by everyone as "Mom." She was a very hard working woman. I sincerely loved her for the person she was. I will always remember her statement about me before she allowed me to marry her daughter, Grace. She said, "He may be short in stature but he is a real man." Sadly, she passed away in August 2010. It was truly an honor to write this poem in her behalf. I read it to her at her retirement dinner on Nov. 10, 1989

Mom Is Always Ready, Mom Is Very Steady

She gets up at the crack of dawn, rubbing her eyes, stretching her
arms and finally yelling out with a loud yawn

Quickly, the hot iron is diligently pressing
a white uniform on her top heavy body neatly caressing

She utters "get up John" another work day, seven to three

Mom is always ready, Mom is very steady

She takes care of sickly bedridden children which is so demanding
her tired feet sometimes gets in the way from hastily walking and
constantly standing

Not complaining if someone should ask, thinking that's petty
she continues to complete her assigned work task

Mom is always ready, Mom is very steady

Bathing, feeding, and changing many a kid
never leaving her various chores undid

Even dealing with an occasional bed-wetty, feverishly working hard
even though she'll never become another J. Paul Getty

She made close friends with patients too
such ones likes Dorothy, there is a quite a few

Mom is always ready, Mom is very steady

A co-worker calling, it might be Eloise, Gladys, Jenette or Evelyn
One of these four is not coming in, leaving the 2nd shift a little bit thin

But, don't worry, it's really no trouble
dependable Mom is willing to pull another double

Mom is always ready, Mom is very steady

Through winter, spring, summer, and fall
year after year, twenty three, overall

Always responding to Lilly's beckon call
Mom was there giving her all and all

It was a happy day when Mom was hired
a sad day now that she is retired

Another Mom will never be found
her associates will be wishing that she was still around

But, don't you fret, because it is a sure bet

that **Mom is always ready, Mom is very steady**

This poetic story is about one of my grandchildren that I wrote in August 2003. His name is Kimball. AKA Chim, Chim. When he was just a little boy, we gave him that nickname. He was always getting into something. Always on the move like a young Chimpanzee. The things he did as a young child was very funny.

Chim, Chim

Right from his early beginning, Kimball was a very lively child
always getting into something, always acting a little crazy and
physically wild

That's why we gladly gave him the nickname, **"Chim, Chim"**
But now, all grown up, he prefers to be identified as just "Kim"

He had the cutest little round face, many a woman did seek, why?
Because their fingers loved to touch and pinch his chubby and
puffy, fat checks

In a car accident with his parents when he was two years old
a small head injury, to the hospital, we thought he be brave and bold

He needed some stitches to patch up his little scalp wound, but soon
as he saw the doctor's needle he screamed and hollered, I guessed he
thought his life was doomed

Poppy and Gram had to hold him down as he struggled and cried
to calm his unfounded fears as the doctor stitched and tied
being there for him, we both certainly took much pride

Like his father Kim was always the ultimate comedian
joking and doings things that caused us & others to mightily
laugh & grin

On vacation in Florida with Asia, Anissa, and Taniera way back when
a condo with a Jacuzzi, he told his sister Asia and cousins to leave
the room, so he can run the water, get butt naked, and promptly jump
right in

Laying his head back in "his" Jacuzzi, as if he had much bling, bling
commanding his humble little slaves to frantically fan him as if
he was their Condo King

When they grew much older we took them on a cruise to
the Bahamas, We could tell Kim was growing into his young
manhood as he smooth talked to many of the ship's young mamas

At age 15, we all know how young ones start to think!
on the ship's bow one evening, someone gave him liquor to drink

On that night we found him behind the ship's theatre movie screen
making silly noises and scaring small children, a startling unruly
scene

When the cruise was finally over, as we all stood in line to debark
a little girl excitedly yelled out, "Mommy, Mommy, there goes
Psycho Man" we all fell out laughing, as Kim surely won over a
little girl fan, and that was his last cruise!

Although he did get himself in a little trouble, he has learned life's
hard knock lessons, he earned his high school diploma and we hope
no more judicial sessions

We all love you, Kim, alias **"Chim, Chim"**, work hard, accomplish
good things as you swim in the ocean of life, keep your head above
torrent waters, we are confident that you will win

This poem I wrote in Jan. 1995. It is dedicated to all the grandparents throughout the world who wholeheartedly & unselfishly give of their time, energy, and love in behalf of their own grandchildren just as my wife and I did.

Grandparent's Love

At an age of forty plus
feels like our years are passing in a rush

Especially, after laboriously raising three darling daughters
My wife and I are retreading old parenting waters

We got granchildren that we certainly adore
four is just enough, hope they don't conceive anymore

Getting up early and transporting them to elementary schools
picking them up, doing homework, I ask myself, are we grandparenting fools?

Reading, writing, & arithmetic
taking care of them even when they become pshycially sick

"Can we spend the night?" is their daily request
Poppy says "maybe" but Gram gives an affirmative "yes"

All of them hyperactive, we never get our well deserved rest
being a granparent really puts our nerves to the ultimate test

Laughter and loud chatter they are constantly engaging
along with ripping, running, and wildly raging

Chim Chim does that, Elizabeth does this, Taniera gleefully always jumping around
And baby Anissa waving her tiny fist
like a cheerleader making goog-ga-ly gog-ga-ly
noises in the background

it's not that we are negatively complaining
rather, in a positive manner merely explaining

What "**grandparent's love**" will painstakingly do
not only for the siblings we personally beared
but, also for our lovely grandchildren too!

This poem was written for my oldest daughter, Claudette, who became part of my life when I married my wife Grace in Oct. 1967. It was difficult enough marrying at a very young age. I was only 18 years old. Taking care of my wife and getting to know her plus with a young child who really did not know me. However, things worked out for the better. Over a short period of time as I learned how to be a real father to her.

My Child

Even though you were not born to me in childbirth, naturally
I took on the role of being your parent, a very difficult & weighty
responsibility

I knew nothing about raising and training a small young child
thinking this situation for me is going to be totally insane and
exceptionally wild

How could I accomplish this parenting feat during my young adult manhood
hoping that you would respond to me favorably and not treat me like
some kind of unworthy wormwood

Early on, when I tried to hold you, you immediately would start to cry
since you did not know me, your perception was that I was an
unidentified bad guy

Over time, I learned how to build a relationship between you and me
we did things together, we bonded, you became part of my marriage family tree

There was no need to adopt you formerly
in my mind and heart you were already **"My Child"** legally

These poems were written for my best friend, my one & only love of my Life.

    This poem was written to my wife back in May 1985. While she was out shopping, I took it upon myself to re-arrange our bedroom, our closet, and dresser items. Which was dominated by her feminine things. And many times everything was in a mess and disorganized. So, here is what I wrote to her to ease her pain when she came home and could not find her personal items in their usual place.

Dear Grace, My Love

Please don't get mad
Or think of me as being bad

I looked at our bedroom
It reminded me of a morbid tomb

All of this dust
In my mind, I really made a big fuss

I thought this room really needs a cleaning porter
To get all of your things in their proper order

Our room really needed a drastic change
So, I took it upon myself to re- arrange

Don't get upset, nothing of yours is misplaced or displaced
All of your Jewelry, cosmetics, and shoes are safe

Just take some time, look in the boxes, you will find
All of the things you need to look pretty and very divine

So in ending, this is my plea
Please! Please! Please!

Don't get mad or think of me as being bad
I hope what I had did will make you feel very glad.

My wife, Grace, is a very energetic person. She always is willing to help others with any type of physical work. Such as cutting grass, planting flowers, cleaning up a yard, etc. This one close female friend of ours needed such assistance back in Aug. 1999. She paid an unexpected physical price for her effort, hard work, & loving assistance. Here is what happened.

The Story of the Unknown Plants

An unfortunate event happened to my wife while she was doing
someone a favor
She was performing much hard work and untold backyard labor

She was cutting their grass and pulling up an unknown plant
& many a weed
Helping another sister out surely was her excelling good deed

But, this unknown plant did not think it was so nice
They said to themselves in their leafy language.
"We are gonna make her pay a very high price."

My wife did not mean it! For she did not know
"It makes no difference" said the unknown plants
"in a few days she will feel the pain, the itching
and the physical woe."

For these unknown plants, you see!
Certainly, did not agree to be pulled up by humans' hands along with
weeds & worthless shrubbery

For this is a warning to the ultimate degree
These unknown plants that your hands may pull up
Just may be, the unknown plant that is called Poison Ivy.

For those of you who are a married man. It may be very hard for you to express your true feelings for your mate verbally. That certainly was the case with me. It was easier for me to express my true feelings of love for my wife, Grace, in written expression, in the form of poetry. So, here is a succession of poems I wrote for her over the many years that we have been married. Many of them were written near the date of our marriage anniversaries.

This is one of the first poems I wrote for her for our 27th Wedding Anniversary

Eventually

Remember the first time that we met?
I was throwing newspapers onto your mother's front step

Although, I didn't know your name
Eventually, I would find out that our initials were exactly the same

A Wilks associated with a White? George and Grace
Eventually, my last name you were destined to willingly embrace

Remember our high school dance?
That surely was the start of our unique romance

I was chosen the Rahway High School King
You joined me on my throne. My heart began to jump and shout!
In my mind I began to sing

Not a fairy tale story or an untrue dream
Eventually, You would become my wifely queen

Remember me driving my father's little blue Covair?
Inviting only you, not your little sister to a social affair

Your mother said, "Leslie is the chaperone."
On no! I didn't want her to tag along
Just wanted it to be, me and my fine lady, all alone!

A stop at the White Castle, Couldn't drive and try to eat
I thought about that little officer sitting in my back seat

Leslie! "Would you hold my food please?"
Eventually, she ate my burgers and then promptly
had the nerve to cop some ZZZ's

That was funny as I think back and laugh
Not having any resentment nor recalling any forgotten rath

Remember that house party? I had too much to drink
Thought I was walking on water!
Eventually, you told me. A bridge over the Rahway River
was the only reason I did not sink

Getting to know you. You getting to know me
Our relationship did not sour. **Eventually**, our loved bloomed!
You became my illustrous "Wild Flower"

Remember asking our parent's permission?
Finally, getting the "go ahead"
Eventually, On Oct. 14, 1967. We both blissfully said
"I take thee, I do wed"

We certainly wasn't among the materially and financially privileged
Could only afford a two room bungalow at Rahway's so-called
Shot-gun Village

Yes, actual shootings, nightly violence, and people were very rough
Eventually, I made "Mo Money". Couldn't wait to getting out
As a southerner would say, "Sho Nuff"

Remember me going to work everyday?
In school one more year you did have to stay

Burn them pots and pans I thought! You did rule
Couldn't wait to get home
Mouth watering, delightful southern home cooked dishes
causing my chops to excessively drool

But, un-be-knownst to me. Your mother was doing the "down home
cookin" And I was played by the sneaky & sly young woman
A broken hearted fool!
Although, several years it did take
Eventually, you became a very fine cook, no longer a fake!
And ummm, them sweet potato pies you really can bake

I could go on. And on. And on, Remembering & telling about our life precious times
past, **Eventually**, I would have to stop. But, I saved the best expression for last

Please listen to these final words I emphatically want to say
"I truly Love You, Grace! Many, many, more times than
once a year on our wedding anniversary day

Love, George Oct. 31, 1994

This poem was written for my wife for our 30th Wedding Anniversary.

Let Me

Let me tell you. Because I want you to know this.
Your womanly charm, your warm embrace, & your passionate kiss
Even after thirty years, your tender love I will never resist

Let me whisper sweet nothings into your ear
And you return to me the favor with pleasant sayings
that I gladly wish to hear

Let me run my steady hand over
your black silvery streaked hair
It is comforting to know that you placed yourself in my loving protective care

Let me continue to share your dreams forever
To fill your heart's desires and
to bring true your life's every endeavor

Let me thank you for our children that you did so willingly bear
And when I pass away from this earth you'll look at their face
& my reflection will aways be there

Let me praise you for the unique woman & wife that you are
intertwined with my mild spirit has brought us good things thus far

Let me thank you for being my dedicated partner in the "truth"
Your "loyal love" compares to a bible character,
the married woman named Ruth.

So, let me take you on a romantic trip if you should dare
We'll have a love treasure that only the two of us will unitedly share

Happy 30th Anniversary

(Love, George Oct. 13, 1997)

This poem was written for my wife for our 35th Wedding Anniversary (this poem was also a song I sang as a surprise for her at our anniversary party).

Talking About My Lady

My lady so peachy sweet
No other woman can compete

My lady is so debonair
I love her silvery streaky hair

My lady has a pretty smile
And her curvy body really drives me wild

My lady really loves to dance
We slow drag making sweet romance

My lady is a joy to be around
She picks me up when I am feeling down

My lady depends on me
I am her man, her solid security

My lady is one of a kind
She's unique, very hard to find

My lady at garage sales
She bargains harder than the average females

Now, you see that lady over there
She is so fine, lovely, black & fair

My lady looks so divine in her clothes
She could've been in many fashion shows

My lady truly inspires me
It's evident, now don't you agree?

Cause, I am Talking about my lady
Talking about my Lady!!!

This poem was written for my wife for our 36th Wedding Anniversary.

My Love For You

My love for you
Is like a river that keeps flowing
My love for you
Is like a full moon that keeps glowing
My love for you
Is like a cherry tree that keeps growing

My love for you
It is true, it is true, it is true

My love For you
Is like rare gold man keep mining

My love for you
Is like the heavenly stars always that keep shining

My love for you
is like a covenant that is always binding

My love for you
It is true, It is true, It is true

This poem was written for my wife, Grace, in regards to her decision to finally retire from work. Her last day of working was May 25, 2012. So, I thought it was nice and appropriate to write her something special.

Constantly Standing

But, now it is your time to slow down, its time to give your energetic
legs and your shuffling feet a much needed rest

Since the early 1970's more than 40 years, all of your jobs demanded
that you work by constantly standing with a whole lot of zest

You proved yourself as an experienced fast food worker, you have more than passed that test

From the days of long ago during our young marriage
working those late night hours at the White Castle

Then, a long work affair with Mr. Burger King & cleaning other
people's houses, those jobs were a time consuming hassle

Next, a short stint employed as a school crossing guard,
again many hours your legs and feet constantly standing
through hot and cold New Jersey weather, you always
displayed a woman working hard

In 2008, moving to Charlotte, seeking out work with some valid fears
again you proved yourself by meeting the challenge and
constantly standing at the Cook Out for about four long years

Learning the ins and the outs, there was no doubt
you would win the approval of your bosses and out working
those Cook Out kids with a whole lot of clout

I'm sure they will miss your hard work ethic, always on the go
and your heartfelt words of encouragement they respected
not forgetting "Miss Grace"
You will always be in their memory which time will never erase

Along with gracefully aging, one's body start to re-arrange
your legs and feet aching & feeling much pain

All that constantly standing, you really had to make a drastic change

So, your retirement is not just about quitting, rather rewarding
yourself, your legs and feet are demanding
time to rest because you always been, constantly standing

So, don't you feel any guilt about your leaving
because it is only very, very fitting
that you take a long, long break and for everybody's sake
to see and say, I saw Miss Grace, she is now finally sitting

Fifty years of marriage is truly a remarkable feat to achieve.

Especially, during these modern times when marriages of today do not last very long. I like to say that my wife and I achieved this special feat despite the many challenges we faced. We married at a very young age. I was eighteen and she was sixteen. Despite that, we both worked together, made compromises, and listened to the wants and cares of each other. And by applying bible principles and guidelines to make our marriage work for the benefit for both of us and our children.

So, I wrote this poem to celebrate our 50th Wedding Anniversary on Oct. 14th 2017, as I took a trip back down memory lane.

Back In Those Days

Back in those days, early in the 1960's, we could buy candy, soda, and ice cream during that time
for no more than a few pennies, or a measly nickel or a dime

At McDonald's or the White Castle, we could buy french fries and
a hamburger or two
the cost was less than twenty five cents each
I remember, because I ate more than a few

Back in those days, the minimum wage was a dollar and forty
cents per hour
The cost of living was much lower than today
and we had much more buying power

Back in those days, the guys wore Winged Tip Shoes, Bell Bottom
dress pants & Shark Skin Suits
We used a chemical cream called Conkalene to make our hair
wavy and shiny to look handsome, suave, and so debonair

We were playing R&B Soul music of the 60's
Going to House Parties was the "in" thing
Doing dances such as the Hitch Hike, Mash Potatoes, the Jerk, the Twist,
the Skate, the Boogaloo, the Shotgun, & the Shing A Ling

Back in those days, the 60's R&B Soul music was simple, pure,
& morally clean
The song lyrics really meant something,
treated men and women with deep respect & much high esteem

Back in Those days, we could buy a 45 inch vinyl record for as little as 69 cents
Portable phonographs
& Eight Track Tape Player sales started to take off and buying those
music playing machines for our cars began to commence

In 1964 & 1965 single records like "My Guy" by Mary Wells and
"My Girl" by the Temptations were number "1" in those years on the
Billboard Hit Charts
We were grooving and singing those R&B hit tunes as the
words of those songs touched and stole our hearts

Back in those days, in 1964, Casius Clay defeated Sonny Liston on
the World Heavy Weight Boxing Championship scene
and three to four years later we were all buying
Johnson Hair Products such as Afro Sheen

Back in those days, early in 1967, I bought my first car
A 1962 Super 88 Oldsmobile
The color was light blue with a convertible white top
the outside and inside was divinely supreme
I was wheeling and dealing, driving on those Rahway, NJ city streets
Y-e-a-h! Curtis Mayfield, I was thankful, diggin the scene
and doing my gangsta lean

Back in those days, gas was only about 33 cents per gallon
It was so, so cheap
I filled up my car's gas tank with the greatest of ease and good maintenance I did keep
Now low gas prices long gone by
what we are paying today, just makes us older folks really want to cry

Y-e-a-h! I was cruising in my Auto-mo-bile! Giving all my close friends rides, that was really cool

Until.....my transmission blew, I bought myself a lemon

I can imagine what that used car
salesman said when I signed on that dotted line, April Fool!
Back to walking during my senior year at Rahway High School

Back in those days, I had a weekend part time job while going
to school and playing high school basketball
But, as a freshman, some of my high school mates said and thought
"he ain't gonna make this team, this little guy is way, way much too short"
However, back in those days, I was very, very quick, ball handling slick,
along with my dribbling, ball stealing and I could really shoot!
Yeah! Their false statements about me now,
became silent and totally mute!

Back in those days, I never boasted about my basketball skills, notoriety, or fame
I was quiet! It was the coaches and the college scouts that really
took notice and raved about my unique game!

And there was someone else interested, it wasn't a secret, Cause when
I played, I saw and heard (this one) screaming out my name
with her lovely dark face
Y-e-a-h! That young woman's identity was my beloved Grace!

Back in those days, I was infatuated with her, she was
infatuated with me! In the meantime, I was offered out of state college
basketball scholarships, I remember the total number was three

Our love for each other grew & grew & grew which was
far more important to me than the latter
My total interest changed, it was re-arranged & marriage was
our foremost subject matter

So, we took that all important next step & exchanged our marriage vows on October 14, 1967
Over the many years our God, Jehovah has given us "solid blessings"
like the manna he gave to the Isrealites that came down from Heaven

So, in harmony with the song that the singing group, The Presidents, sang in 1962
Lasting Forever, from, 5, 10, 15, 20, 25, 30 yrs of love,
now 50 years for me and you.

My wife & me at our 50th wedding anniversary
with some of our immediate family members
(In the Background) Evelyn, Claudette, Tamika & Michael

Grace & Me standing at the anniversary table
Cutting the unique 50th wedding anniversary cake
made to look like a vinyl record because we love
to dance to the 60's, 70's, & 80's R& B Soul music

On many occasions, I wrote poems for some of my friends and close associates. Some poems were written for their wedding anniversaries, persons that were moving far away, and when family members have lost a loved one in death. They want to have a written memory of them and want to express how they truly felt for that particular person.

So, here are some of those poems.

This poem was written for a couple for their wedding day.

You Are My Sun, I am The Rain

You are my Sun
And I am the Rain

Making our love grow together
without any burden or pain

That which aids our love to mature
is your rays of womanly charm

No chill will ever set in
No elements will hinder or bring our love any harm

Showers of praises,
compliments, I reward thee

Our marriage reaping many benefits
Reminiscent of a fruit bearing tree

Your hand in mine
United as one

Forever we will be
I am the Rain
And you are my Sun

This poem was written for a special couple for their 40th wedding anniversary as a surprise wedding gift for them. It is a poetic true life story about both of them leading up to their marriage.

Shelly Became Ron's Ribbon In The Sky

In Louisiana is where Ronny Granvel's life did start
born into his parents large family shopping cart

Five brothers and four sisters, the total number of his siblings
not a wealthy family coming from very humble southern beginnings

As Ron grew up being very studious & smart in
elementary & high school
he also had a physical attribute which may have caused
high school coaches to excessively drool

As he physically grew from year to year, way over six feet tall
I am very sure high school coaches tried to recruit him
to play the game of basketball

However, if he did play that sport on an organized level,
it wasn't his goal
It was Jehovah's Witnesses & bible truth that was secured
in his mind, heart, & soul

It was an associate, brother Henderson, who studied with Ron
on a steadfast regular basis
Yes, the truth took a definite hold
and spiritual goals he readily embraces

He was the only one in his large family clan
to dedicate himself to serve Jehovah,
he fulfilled his initial spiritual game plan

So, in the year 1974, the truth was already a solid stronghold
at the ripe age of 19 he was invited to Brooklyn Bethel,
a new found threshold

Now let's transition our thoughts to a family located way up north
The Harden family, always taking trips to Brooklyn Bethel
from New Jersey, going back and forth

Two boys and a girl, their mother firmly established in the "Truth"
teaching and training her children all the while during their youth

Sylvia's lovely daughter which we all know, her name is Shelly
Her mother put a colorful ribbon in her curly hair
right after she came out of Momma Harden's birth belly

It is said, Shelly loved to wear large ribbons in her hair
for 15 years of more
It would be hard for anyone not to notice
that ribbon hair style that she constantly wore

Sister Harden and her three teenage children taking
another educational tour
to Brooklyn Bethel visiting the office complex, the factory,
and making many Bethel friends, that was for sure

A personal guide allowed Momma Harden to cross over a yellow
book binding safety line
Not to inspect the literature, it was Ron, tall, dark, & handsome,
what an immaculate find!
A possible husband for Shelly! That was her thinking
in her motherly matchmaking mind

Soon after that, Ron & his Bethelite brothers traveled to Newark,
located in the Garden State

Invited to Shelly's party, the first step leading up to
a possible engagement date

From then on, Ron was making regular trips from Bethel
to see Shelly at her home
when they went out together, her younger Brother, Darren,
was designated to be the honorary chaperone

Ron getting to know Shelly and Shelly getting to know him,

Barry & Sylvia Harden knew that their relationship was lighting up!
Their love for each other would grow & grow, never to become dim!
It may have been in the month of February of the year 1978
Ron asked Barry's permission to marry his daughter, but it was
Sylvia Harden, from that very first meeting,
had already sealed their romantic fate

Living at Bethel during the 70's, the monetary allowance
was very, very small
to make some extra money, there was a golden opportunity
that Ron may surely recall

Painting Carrie Coleman's living room, a job he completed
really very, very nice
He knew he had to do it well
just in case he had to pay a small token brideprice!

So, Ron asked Shelly to marry him and she gleefully said an overwhelming yes!
There was no engagement ring but Shelly said to Ron, that's OK
Ron was planning to purchase one & present it to her on
another special day

After a memorial celebration, sitting at a restaurant dinner table
Ron ask Shelly to take a ring off her finger, if she was able

He easily slipped the engagement ring on,
No reaction from his bride to be, was she so surprised,
or couldn't speak or was something unexpectedly wrong?

I am sure Ron was amazed & dazzed! As they
both ate and finished their dinner
cause Shelly still didn't realize that something brand new was on
her left hand ring finger!

As ladies always do, a need to refresh themselves in a restroom
All of a sudden loud screams of joy came from Shelly, as she finally
looked down to feast her eyes on the
engagement ring from her soon to be elated bridegroom

So on Nov. 18, 1978, Ron & Shelly became husband & wife,
a beautiful Kingdom Hall wedding, a reception & a nice honeymoon
Afterwards, Ron ushered his new bride into
Brooklyn Bethel's full time servants glorious life

You might say that Shelly became Ron's "Ribbon In The Sky"
if you listen to the lyrics of Stevie Wonder's beautiful love song,
one and all will certainly know the very reason why!

My Only Lady, My Lovely Bride

I remember the day when we first met
June 19, 1961 that year I will never forget

While Painting in my Uncles's house
In Claxton Georgia, way down in the deep south

My cousin introduced you to me, Leila is your name
That social event started a spark, a spark of interest
that eventually turned into a glowing love flame

Even though I liked the way you looked
It was your inner beauty and your lovely smile, Yes that
That is what really got me hooked

Easy to talk to, your sayings very smooth and mild
Pleasant to be with, not man hungry or worldly wild

Being in the military service, at times, I had to say a sad goodbye
However, your loyalty and trust, I knew that I could surely rely

Two years passing, our love was in constant bloom
I thought to myself, would she take me as her only man
to become her bridegroom?

Always writing you, Wanting to be by your grateful side
Wondering if you were willing to be **My Only Lady, My Lovely Bride**

Written proposal of marriage in my trembling hand
One for you and your parents too!
Hoping they'll let me take their daughter's life
in my gentle command

My heart jumping with excitement, couldn't sleep or rest
But, finally an answer, they didn't protest
And best of all, **You** gave me a definite **yes!**

So on December 22nd in the year 1962
We sealed our marriage vows with the words "I Do"

24 years living on Fulton Street
Along came Sharon & Laura, our family was complete

Although 30 years have passed
Some things I will always treasure
Things that are etched in my mind forever

That is your inner beauty, your lovely smile
Taking care of the children all the while,
being patient and strong, and putting up with me
even when I did some wrong

I am glad you became **My Only Lady,**
My Lovely Bride, I am telling the world,
My love for you, I will never, never, Hide

What Can I say About Jesse & Pam?

First of all, they have been married for twenty six fulfilling years
much longer than many of their close associates and their peers

They lived in New Jersey, in the city of Bayonne
They never had any children, my guess is that their joy is to be
"home alone"

Jesse is a dedicated husband, a mild mannered, quiet kind of person,
and a very understanding man
Which are very good positive qualities he surely does command

Pam is very lively, she adds the "Spice" as Jesse's immaculate partner
and loving wife
As they both serve Jehovah together in this uncertain earthly life

Pam's sister told me that Pam loved to imitate Elvis Presley & his songs
of "Rock n Roll"
She was always playing his vinyl records, singing & dancing "to and fro"

That was the start of many different dances that Pam really can do
Herein, I like to name just a few
She can Mash Potatoes, she can do the Slop,
She can Funky Chicken or do the Wop

Pam can do the dance of the 1940's which is called the "The Jitterbug"
Nothing has changed over the many years
As we all can attest, Pam can still "Cut A Rug"

She is so quick and light on her feet, everyone loves to watch her do
her "Own Thing."
She is just like her father, I can just see both of them doing that
dance called the "The Swing"

However, Pam's feet was not used just for mere pleasure
She was a Regular Pioneer for about twenty years
A service to Jehovah that she will always treasure

And I heard about Jesse, how he was very good in playing the
game of high school basketball
How the college recruiters came calling, constantly knocking at his door

They admired his style and his polished game
Now, they were begging for more and more

But, it was to no avail, their offers, Jesse did not entertain
Like Moses, in turning down the Egyptian worldly riches
Jesse courageously choose the "Truth" which was a far much better gain

Even though Jesse's basketball days have all but diminished
He is now playing the more important "Spiritual Game"

Right down to the final minute of the last quarter he is winning!
Jehovah will surely remember, not only his number,
but more importantly his name

For thirty years Jesse & Pam were associated with
the Bayonne Kingdom Hall
Now that they are leaving, I think! The Brothers should etch their
names into the 44th street Kingdom Hall "Walls"

So now, as another chapter of Jesse's and Pam's life began
On their way to Atlanta, Georgia
I am sure they will be making many more new friends

However, let them not forget all the memories and your grateful
"down home Brothers & Sisters" from the early beginnings

Our "Love" for both of you will be "forever" as this segment
of your lives has a glorious farewell ending

To My Wife From Earl

You are the sole reason for my wanting to live
I would be lost without you, a wandering man, perhaps even a fugitive

You make me feel like there is nothing that I can not do
you support me and keep my spirits alive, fresh and anew

And when I'm feeling "down" and not thinking too straight
you are right there "uplifting" me like a loving magistrate

You make me feel that there is everything to keep trying for
your "unconditional love" I will cherish evermore

I know that if I had not met you six years ago
Right now! My life would have been a mess and nothing good to show

I realized that I loved you and needed you to be part of my life
I thank Jehovah I made the right decision & asked you to
become my wife

It's been wonderful, these six years of marriage that we have spent
Just as Jehovah has said, a woman such as you is truly a compliment

Loving, understanding, caring, unselfish and always sharing

If I were a cup of coffee you would definitely be the sugar in me
Forevermore is my love, happy anniversary to my wife, Jackie.

Inner Beauty & Inner Qualities

It wasn't his physical attraction that captured me
Rather his "inner beauty" was the dominant key

Through all of our wonderful & glorious forty three years
No need for me to dread or to have any negative fears

A good husband and family provider, he fulfilled his responsibility
He did that to the ultimate degree

A loving, unselfish, and a patient man
He never made an unreasonable demand

His kindness, his goodness, and the joy that we shared
These "inner qualities" really showed me that he truly cared

Together in my heart that's where Jess and I will always be
Even though he is gone in death he is still very, very close to me

As he lay to rest, to all I make this proclaim
My love for Jess will be an eternal burning flame

A Wedding Anniversary Poetry Gift For Simon & Kattie Priester

A number of worldly historical events took place during the
year of 1940 that made international headline news

Germany invaded Norway & Denmark
Winston Churchill became the British Prime Minister

Germany also attacks Belgium, Holland, & France
and the Swing is still a major hot dance

I wonder were both of you, on the floor together, doing that dance
Simon and Kattie is having a whirlwind oldtime romance

FM Radio hit the worldly scene, Frank Sinatra made his singing
debut with the Tommy Dorsey Orchestra
Did his crooning make Kattie scream?

The battle of Great Britain begins & Germany losses
FDR was re-elected as President of the United States
for a record third time
You could read all about it in Life Magazine which cost only a dime

Race Riots in Chicago, Los Angeles, Detroit & Harlem
Afro-Americans making a real big fuss
I wonder did you and Kattie have to sit in the back of the bus?

A cartoon character named Woody Wood Pecker first appeared
World War is on the horizon, many a people sadly feared

And Leana Horne was a very glamorous hot chick
But in that year, Simon Priester, chose a pretty little woman named
Kattie to be his wife and a life long sidekick

Shirley Temple made her 44th movie entitled "The Blue Bird"
She was only twelve years old

Simon was twenty one & Kattie was twenty
Start of a marriage solid as gold

Charlie Chaplin ridicules Hitler in the movie, "The Great Dictator"
Walt Disney created the Animated movie entitled "Fantasia"

Did both of you see those movies as a theater spectator?
The average price was only about a quarter

In 1940 the production of the first Jeep
I wonder what you were driving, Simon,
was it an old jalopy heap?

You could have bought a brand new Cadillac Sedan for $1,750
or a new Dodge for a $1,000 less, it would only cost you $750

The average worker's wage was about 30 cents per hour
It really didn't matter how much you made cause your money
in those days had great buying power

It is nice to think back about worldly events, good times,
and bad times to remember
day to day, month to month, from January to December

But, to remember that special day on August 28th, 1940
when both of you said your "I Do's"
It may have not made headline news

However, your marriage is secured with Jehovah, more solid than cement
Sixty Seven years of marriage longevity is truly worthy of being
a historical international headline news event

This poem was written one night during our first seven day cruise on board Royal Caribbean's wonderful ship, Sovereign of the Seas December 2-9, 1995.

Sovereign of the Seas Cruise Vacation

We were cruisin' on the ship called Sovereign of the Seas
Strolling on the decks and coolin' in the breeze
as we traveled warm waters of Caribbean Sea

From the Port of Miami our ship was set free
as we headed for the Island of renewed Haiti
Had a good time on an island beach resort
called Labadee, Labadee

We were rockin' and a reelin'
Our tummies got a squeezy feelin'
Not spoiling our vacation while the ship's flirtation
with all those ocean waves, ocean waves

We were touring and exploring, on board playing games
some tried and gained their fame
there was laughter and holla!
We won all those Ship Shape Dollars, Ship Shape Dollars

Many times dressing up formal, it just ain't normal
But, we didn't mind cause the waiter service
was real darn fine, real darn fine!

When the ship's bell chimes, we ate a lotta times
all the food was tastin' goody
Sweets and treats, everything was tooty fruity

Our tummies said its like taking the booty,
taking the booty

All the ports of call, the island Puerto Rico
St. Thomas beckons as part of this sea sequel
as we made our way to the bay of Cococay, Cococay

Although our cruise is certainly not over
The Sovereign of the Seas is a Super Nova
To the Captain and the Crew, just to name a few
We like to say Thank you, Thank you

This next poem I wrote after experiencing a horrific event that I watched on live TV from the news media. An event that affected every American soul on the morning of Sept. 11, 2001.

First One, Then the Other
(Sept. 16, 2001)

A calamitous event that I will always remember in the picture
of my mind's eye that will never be undone
It happened on a Tuesday morning, the 11th day of September 2001

Getting ready for work was my foremost intent
Then a news flash came across my tv screen, "Attack on America",
caused my eyes and ears to be fixated and bent

Sounds of roaring jet engines swooping down like giant birds of prey
First one, then the other, their targets in sight on two twin
towers, one hundred and ten story brothers

These two buildings known as New York City's World Trade Center
Where thousands of business people work and tourist daily enter

Foreign terrorist guiding these giant mechanical birds which
harbored their hate
Uncanny planning, four passenger jet airplanes they did
hijack from Boston & Newark airport gates

Headed for the Pentagon and the White House included as targets
as the FBI found out later on this unprecedented historic date

Like guided missles hurling themselves, zeroing in on their prey
First one, then the other
Explosions turn into gapping holes on each building; so much
damage, then fire & smoke
My eyes swell up, I felt myself tremble, my heart is almost in my throat

Thousands of innocent people are caught so unaware
The news media, many eyewitnesses, and television viewers, including myself are befuddled
A feeling of great anger and utter despair
There is nothing anyone could do, but just shutter with a horrified stare

So many lives trapped inside these two huge towering infernos
Firemen and medical personnel rush to the scene as this
true life castastrophic event unfolds

And then, the unthinkable, to my eyes dreadful surprise
These two seemingly, invincible monumental structures with
all of its financial enterprise

Within fifteen minutes between the two towers
First one, then the other
starts to disintegrate in a furious tumble, forming dark
mushroom clouds of dust & ticker tape debris
All of lower Manhattan has experienced a major cataclysmic catastrophe

Almost five thousand human lives buried among the twisted, mangled metal, and concrete
Resembling a war torn city with other buildings, vehicles, &
communications dashed to pieces all over downtown New York City streets
Memories of Pearl Harbor is unleashed as this tragic wicked
deed became so complete

Men of authority promises to bring retaliation and vengeance upon
those responsible for this carnage on that unforgettable day
However, men can't bring back the lives of loved ones,
family members, and friends

It is only wise to look to our God, Jehovah, who will bring true justice and comfort
He is the only one that will definitely make amends

Coronavirus Known as Covid-19

From the depths of Wuhan, a Chinese capital city,
a deadly disease came on the worldly scene

In March of the year of 2020, a given name of Coronavirus
known as Covid-19

Chinese medical doctors tried to control it and limit its spread
before they even knew it, Chinese people got infected
and now many of them are sadly dead

Because of mankind's global travel, this novel virus
hitched an international ride

And began to infect and contaminate millions of people
in a matter of months going worldwide

This person to person airborne transmitted disease
wreaked havoc on leisure cruise line travel
throughout the ocean's great seven seas

Many ports of call were officially shut down
as cruise passengers had to stay on board
ships just sitting still in ocean waters, and anchors were all aground

Nursing homes became heavy Coronavirus hot spots
as the elderly were easy targets to contract this disease
sending many of the aged to unwanted human grave plots

Corporations, small businesses, & all restaurant places
governments & cities making it mandatory to work at home, no dining out
as doctors & scientists do vaccine research & testing, covering all of their bases

An international job loss, many are unemployed
an economic downturn, the Coronavirus originated this ugly financial void

Throughout the whole world, travel on airplanes, buses & trains
was on hold as the Coronavirus is causing many stresses, heartaches, and pains

No roaring team favorites sitting in crowded bleacher stands
all types of sporting games & events, they all were affected
as the Coronavirus amended their seasonal plans

NBA Basketball didn't experience hardly any Coronavirus trouble
as playoffs and championship games where played in Orlando, Florida's
well secured and protective so-called "Bubble"

Some GOP Republican officials & President Trump falsely stated:
"many people will not get Covid-19, the news media, Dr. Fauci, & CDC
scientist are wrong, their fact filled predictions are highly over-rated"

However, all ages of humans are not immune to contracting Covid-19
including the Donald, He got it too! Along with almost nine million
people, he was treated & immediately quarantined

All elementary schools, colleges, & universities initially shutdown
no students or teachers
all educational facilities resembled a learning ghost town

And now, our administrators requesting our children to go back to a classroom much too soon?
Still, the Coronavirus is hovering over them
causing parents much anxiety, thinking their precious child eventually may be doomed

44 million worldwide cases and over one million deaths, a spiraling epidemic
over 225,000 US lives taken from us up to this present October 2020 date
more and more humans souls will be lost by this prolific pandemic

Many protective mask are worn, staying six feet apart, even though some complain
the breath of life is still taken away, the Coronavirus known as Covid-19
presently is still not being constrained

George Wilks
Oct. 27, 2020

This is poem was written for and dedicated to some of my elderly Jehovah Witness associates in the South English Congregation located in Elizabeth, New Jersey. Many of them have passed away, but their fine examples of faithful service despite physical trials and tribulations will always be in my mind's eye & deeply touched my heart. (September 9, 2000)

Appreciating the "Elderly Ones"

As the bible says, "grey headedness is a crown of beauty"
I am not repeating those words just to display a sense
of an Elder's duty

Because, I have seen the "Elderly Ones" perform a variety of
good works over many years
And I have dealt with some of their worries and even some of
their worst fears

Despite their physical ailments, many aches and many a pain
They continue to serve Jehovah faithfully
and not utter a plaintiff cry or constantly complain

I remember when Simon Priester developed a cataract in his eye
It didn't dampen his willing spirit to continue to serve
On his God, Jehovah he surely did rely

And look at Mattie Belvin, way up in age by far
Using a crutch just to take a step, but she is regular at our meetings
and in the field service, she truly is an Elderly shining star

Dorothy Ross, a small woman in physical stature,
but she possesses a great big heart
She puts forth so much effort to be at the meetings and in the field ministry
I know that she is always willing to do her part

Recently Kattie Priester received an accidental burn on her neck & chest
Things like these that befall "Eldery Ones" can cause so
much pain & stress

That physical setback didn't allow her joy to serve Jehovah
to become unraveled & regress

Some of our "Elderly Ones" had lost close loved ones
in the sting of death
Such as Louis Palmer, Vernon Weeks, Arona Williams,
& the Ramdeems

However, they didn't allow that to affect their service because each
of them know Jehovah's promise of a resurrection is not just a dream

Brother & Sister Metrokiewcz experienced physical and mental
persecution in Europe they did go through
They are a fine testimony of not giving in
Their faith & integrity in Jehovah certainly proved true

To Emma Stokes and Gladys Jones, I quote these bible words
"I know your deeds"
Picking up your elderly companion sisters for the meetings &
field ministry, they did go
What a fine service that both of you do for others
Jehovah, he too, is very much in the know

There are those, who, in so many other fine ways,
continue to remain steadfast
Such as our dear elderly single sister, Lorene Nash

These examples are just some samples of what the "Elderly Ones" are
doing to prove their worth
And I, for one, appreciate their efforts, learn from their fine examples
and look forward to serving with them when they are
"young again"
in Jehovah God's everlasting new earth

A Living Trophy I will be

In an approved state I shall be
when God Triumphs in victory
A survivor! Shouting with glee
A living trophy I will be

For without spot and not even a blemish
when God's victory is finally finished
A survivor! Not just a refugee
A living trophy I will be

No pain, nor death, or misery
finally an end to Satan's Trickery
and then a great jubilee
Happily proclaiming by a decree
A living trophy I will be

Pouring Rains of Blessings

Pouring rains of blessings
there will prove to be
No cause to have thirst
Life's waters forevermore is free

Pouring rains of blessings
upon the weary field
No cause to have hunger
the land will always give its yield

Pouring rains of blessings
to undo fermented poverty
A cause for proclaiming
a perfect everlasting novelty

Pouring rains of blessings
upon a jubilant rebirth
Once a polluted world
Now! A rejuvenated paradise earth

The Holder of Our Existence Deed

The holder of our existence deed
gives us power and courage to always succeed

Don't feel ashamed for doing your Christ-like best
remember his actions when undergoing trial like test

Hold on to your faith and integrity too
Jehovah, our God, will surely reward you if you constantly do

Let a tear not drop from your dreary eyes
nor feel regrets let none of them arise

depend upon our God all your earthly days
as you continue to walk in his righteous ways

Because he is the one, like a motherly Dove
helping us as his children, always showing tender mercy and love

Because he is the one, the holder of our existence deed
always call upon him whenever in dire need

My Eyes

The color of the sky
to gaze upon the starry night

The beauty of a rose
its red color so clear upon my sight

Different shades of people
my eyes do apprehend

Such varieties of color
to earth did our Creator extend

But, what are these
to a person born blind?

How can one picture them
in their darkened mind?

For what price one would pay?
Just to see, for one instance of a day

To experience color
desiring nothing more

Such an exquisite treasure
for one's eyes forever to store

Is this sense of sight
taken for granted that I possess?

No! sincere gratitude
and its magnificence I will always manifest

Summer Breeze

Listening intently
to its whispering sound

Invisible to one's sight
but acutely aware that it's around

A character of nature
with all of its finesse

causing trivial object
to come alive & unrest

slowly and surely
like the leaves on a limb

all becomes eloquently quiet
thinking, it's finally dim

but, unexpectingly to one's senses
it rallies and commences

Suddenly with such great ease
an oncoming summer breeze

Feverish Free Flight

Fluttering feathers in the sky
riding the wind so very high

Body sleek, long or slender
yearning to be free, never to surrender

nothing to bind like a desolate kite
forever to be in feverish free flight

only hunger and thirst
betokens rest for a minute

so far, so far.......
only earth boundaries are its limit

Rushing Waves

The commutive masses of mankind
resemble the rushing waves of the sea
upon the ever waiting vastness of the shore

As though hearing craving love calls from its mate
the sounds of roaring engines beckons
them to the affair before its too late

And very discreet to one's attentive ear
the echoing thunder of congested feet
like a human herd stampeding in fear

"All aboard" a shouting conductor's command
a last look or two, no one standing
not even a few

Onward locomotive until your next stop
for the rushing waves of passengers are forever due

Clouds

Like oceans stemming from a gentle flowing river
or a virgin stream

Towering as if majestic mountains
molding a concentrated aeronautic team

Cirrus, Nimbus, and Stratus
Just to name of few

Constantly changing their ambiguous structure
forming watery vapors anew

To marvel at this unequaled creation upon one's sight
Appearing fluffy, soft, pure and so elegantly white

Earth's never ending protective shrouds
these amazing jewels called clouds

Chim Chim, the Condo King

They will read poetry that tells about family relationships, people, & their life's experiences. They will appreciate the wonderful things our creator made to bring humans much pleasure. They will appreciate the unique way that poetry is used to tell true stores about people and their true feelings for others.

Printed in the United States
By Bookmasters